Magical Miracle™

CONTENTS

Circle of Friends

Magical Miracle

Volume 4

By

Yuzu Mizutani

HAMBURG // LONDON // LOS ANGELES // TOKYO

Magical x Miracle Volume 4

Created By Yuzu Mizutani

Translation - Yoohae Yang
English Adaptation - Mark Ilvedson
Copy Editor - Stephanie Duchin
Retouch and Lettering - Star Print Brokers
Production Artist - Bowen Park
Graphic Designer - James Lee

Editor - Hope Donovan
Digital Imaging Manager - Chris Buford
Pre-Production Supervisor - Erika Terriquez
Art Director - Anne Marie Horne
Production Manager - Elisabeth Brizzi
Managing Editor - Vy Nguyen
VP of Production - Ron Klamert
Editor-in-Chief - Rob Tokar
Publisher - Mike Kiley
President and C.O.O. - John Parker
C.E.O. and Chief Creative Officer - Stuart Levy

TOKYOPOP and [logo] are trademarks or registered trademarks of TOKYOPOP Inc.

TOKYOPOP Inc.
5900 Wilshire Blvd. Suite 2000
Los Angeles, CA 90036

E-mail: info@TOKYOPOP.com
Come visit us online at www.TOKYOPOP.com

MAGICAL X MIRACLE © 2005 by Yuzu Mizutani. All rights reserved. First published in Japan in 2005 by ICHIJINSHA, Tokyo. English translation rights in the United States of America and Canada arranged with ICHIJINSHA.

English text copyright © 2007 TOKYOPOP Inc.

All rights reserved. No portion of this book may be reproduced or transmitted in any form or by any means without written permission from the copyright holders. This manga is a work of fiction. Any resemblance to actual events or locales or persons, living or dead, is entirely coincidental.

ISBN: 978-1-59816-331-5

First TOKYOPOP printing: April 2007

10 9 8 7 6 5 4 3 2 1

Printed in the USA

Magical
× Miracle
4
水谷悠珠
YUZU MIZUTANI

Character Introductions

VAITH

A LOYAL FOLLOWER OF THE MASTER WIZARD AS WELL AS CAPTAIN OF THE BLACK KNIGHTS. HANDSOME AND DECEPTIVELY SMOOTH.

MERLEAWE

A BRAVE YOUNG GIRL WHO AGREES TO POSE AS THE MISSING SYLTHFARN UNTIL HE CAN BE FOUND. BOTH POSITIVE AND CHEERFUL, SHE IS DETERMINED TO MAKE THIS MOST UNUSUAL MISSION A SUCCESS!

FERN

ANOTHER DISCIPLE OF THE MASTER WIZARD. BECAUSE HE IS FROM A HAHZE FAMILY, HE HAS AN UNUSUALLY STRONG RESISTANCE TO MAGICAL SPELLS.

GLENN

IN ADDITION TO SERVING THE MASTER WIZARD, THIS SWEET PRIEST PROVIDES EDUCATION TO MANY OF THE TOWN'S CHILDREN.

YUE

THE UNDERSECRETARY OF THE MAGIC DEPARTMENT, HE CONSIDERS IT HIS DUTY TO BE VERY STRICT WITH EVERYONE ELSE.

PRINCESS SERAPHIA

SHE IS BOTH PRINCESS OF VIEGALD AND FIANCÉE TO SYLTHFARN.

STORY

JUST AS SHE BEGAN TO STUDY MAGIC, MERLEAWE WAS CALLED UPON TO POSE AS SYLTHFARN, THE MASTER WIZARD OF THE KINGDOM OF VIEGALD, SINCE SHE BEARS SUCH A STRIKING RESEMBLANCE TO HIM. CAUGHT UP IN A WORLD SHE DOES NOT KNOW, SHE NOW STRUGGLES TO DO HER BEST WITH THE FULL SUPPORT OF SYLTHFARN'S FOLLOWERS. BUT NOW, DESPITE MEL'S BEST EFFORTS, PRINCESS SERAPHIA HAS BEGUN TO SUSPECT THAT SHE HAS BEEN BETRAYED BY AN IMPOSTER...

SYLTHFARN

THE MASTER WIZARD OF VIEGALD. STILL MISSING.

I MUST FIND OUT!
I KNOW THAT I'M RIGHT!
WHAT'S GOT YOU SMILING, GLENN?
WELL!
I'M ABOUT TO TRY A NEW TEA.
WOULD YOU CARE TO JOIN ME?
?
STOMP STOMP STOMP STOMP

Episode.25

ぱッ

WHERE IS...

...SYLTH ?!

んっ

HUH?

PRINCESS SERAPHIA?

I WASN'T INFORMED YOU PLANNED ON VISITING TODAY.

When did you decide--?

きょろきょろ

WHAT IN THE WORLD IS GOING ON HERE?!

THAT ROOM MUST BE HIS!

ばた

んっ

......
からっ

WHAT'S GOING ON, SERAPHIA?
SIT ON A TACK THIS MORNING?

ARE YOU ALL...
...BLIND?

きくっ!

THE MAN YOU'VE BEEN CALLING THE MASTER WIZARD...
...ISN'T THE REAL SYLTH-FARN AT ALL!
!!!
NOW YOU HAD BETTER TELL ME WHERE HE IS RIGHT NOW!
H-HE...
IS SHE SERIOUS?
HE'S WORK-ING...

I DIDN'T ASK YOU ABOUT WHAT...
...HE'S DOING.
ずいっ
I DEMAND TO KNOW WHERE HE IS!
DO YOU UNDER-STAND ME?

HE, UH, HE'S...

NEVER MIND.
I SHALL GO ASK YUE.

OH NO!
I BELIEVE YUE'S TUTORING MERLEAWE AT THIS VERY MOMENT!

PRINCESS SERAPHIA.
RATTLE
PLEASE SIT DOWN. I WILL GO AND FIND OUT HIS SCHEDULE AT ONCE.
...THANK YOU.
GOOD THINKING, GLENN!

UM...

I'VE JUST BREWED A NEW TEA.

Would you care to try?

Don't waste my time...

...with small talk!!

Eek!

UM...

...IS THIS RIGHT?

GUYS! WE'RE IN BIG TROUBLE!
PRINCESS SERAPHIA SUSPECTS THE TRUTH!
SHE'S COMING TO SEE YOU!
...
WHAT?

ABOUT SYLTH-FARN!
EH?!
THE PRINCESS KNOWS EVERY-THING!
I DON'T KNOW HOW, BUT SHE DOES!
たったっ
Uh... Uh...
...!
~~~?!!

GLENN'S DETAINED HER IN HIS ROOM RIGHT NOW. BUT SHE'LL BE HERE ANY MINUTE!
What am I going to do?!
I SEE.

I WILL SPEAK TO HER.
FERN, TAKE MERLEAWE SOMEWHERE SAFE AND KEEP HER HIDDEN.
~~~

AH!
MEL!
WE'VE GOTTA GET OUT OF HERE!
OKAY.
COME ON!
LET'S GO SEE VAITH!
......
NOW...
...WHAT SHALL I SAY?
sigh...

YUE!
WELCOME, PRINCESS.
YOU MUST HAVE SOMETHING OF GREAT IMPORTANCE TO DISCUSS, SEEING AS YOU CAME ALL THIS WAY...
...without any notice?
YES!

REMEM-
BER.
YOU NEED BOTH PHYSICAL AND MENTAL STRENGTH.

AND--
AH.
"AH"?

SORRY! I NEED TO BORROW HIM FOR A LITTLE WHILE!
URK!

THAT WAS THE MASTER WIZARD!
AND OUR LEADER HAS BEEN KIDNAPPED!

MEN! I EXPECT YOU ALL TO DO TWO HUNDRED MORE SIT-UPS AND PUSH-UPS AND THEN WORK ON YOUR SQUATS FOR 20 MINUTES!
Get moving!
THAT'S FIVE SETS!
YES, SIR...

WHAT'S GOING ON?
Whew...
This is getting...
...ridiculous!
I WAS HARD AT WORK.
THING IS...
ごにょごにょ

WHAT?!
THAT'S NO GOOD AT ALL!

EXACTLY. HOW SHOULD WE RESOLVE THIS?
UM...

......

I...
...DON'T WANT TO KEEP RUN-NING.

HUH?
WHAT ARE YOU SAYING?

FIRST, WE LIED TO HER.

AND NOW WE'RE ABOUT TO RUN AWAY FROM THE TRUTH AGAIN?

WE CAN'T DO THAT TO HER.

THE PRINCESS IS ONLY EIGHT YEARS OLD.

AND SHE IS SO PURE.

SHE LOVES...
...THE MASTER WIZARD SO VERY MUCH!
I THINK WE OWE HER AN EXPLANATION.
I CAN'T DECEIVE HER ANYMORE.
LOUD AND CLEAR.
LET'S GO SEE HER.
WHAT? VAITH?!

ふるふるふる
...WE ALL KNOW SHE CAN BE AWFULLY STUBBORN.
HER
ALL RIGHT.

LET'S HOPE YUE'S PLANNED FOR THIS CONTINGENCY.
SINCE HE'S SUCH A WORRYWART AND ALL.

VAITH?!

Tch.

FINALLY, YOU'RE HERE!

I WOULD LIKE TO SPEAK AT ONCE.

THE FLOWER THAT SYLTH OFFERED ME THAT VERY FIRST TIME...

AH!

THAT'S FROM OUR LAST VISIT!

...WAS NOT THIS ONE.

SO I'M THE ONE THAT GOOFED...

AND SO I KNOW THAT...
...YOU ARE NOT SYLTH-FARN.

EVEN MASTER WIZARDS GET CONFUSED ABOUT STUPID GIRLY DETAILS EVERY ONCE IN A WHILE.
NO, SYLTH HAS NEVER FORGOTTEN ANYTHING OR MADE SUCH A CARELESS MISTAKE!
I SHOULDN'T HAVE TO TELL YOU THAT.
URK...
OH MAN.
FOR-GIVE ME...
...PRIN-CESS.
WE CAN'T LIE TO HER ANYMORE!
YOU'RE RIGHT. I'M NOT THE MASTER WIZARD.

ふらっ
I...!
ふわっ
MEL!
YOU'RE ...
...A GIRL?!
へたっ..

PRINCESS, I APOLOGIZE.
I'M THE ONE RESPONSIBLE.
SO YOU ARE THE ONE WHO DECEIVED ME...
...YUE?
TELL ME, WHERE IS SYLTH?
HE HAS BEEN MISSING FOR SIX MONTHS NOW.

SO YOU SET THIS UP WITHOUT OUR...

YOU ALL TOOK PART IN THIS?!

WHY DIDN'T YOU JUST TELL ME THE TRUTH?

I WAS HOPING TO FIND SYLTHFARN BEFORE THERE WAS ANY CAUSE FOR ALARM.

I DIDN'T WANT TO WORRY OUR KING, OR YOU, PRINCESS.

SO YOU WERE TRYING TO PROTECT THE COUNTRY?
IT IS, I ADMIT, A FEEBLE EXCUSE.
YOU BLATANTLY LIED TO MY GRANDFATHER AND ME!
......

NO! I DON'T WANT TO DISCUSS IT ANY-MORE.
ANYWAY...
WHO IS THIS GIRL?

MEL CAME FROM THE COUNTRY-SIDE TO STUDY MAGIC.
IT WAS FATE THAT I HAPPENED TO STUMBLE UPON HER.
WHAT?!

YOU GAVE ALL THIS RESPONSIBILITY TO AN ORDINARY CITIZEN WHO KNOWS NOTHING OF OUR WORLD?!
SUCH CRUEL PEOPLE YOU ALL ARE!!
ふわっ...
YOU MUST HAVE BEEN...
...SO FRIGHTENED BY ALL OF THIS.

I...
I...
I SHOULD SAY...
...SOMETHING!
...
THIS IS THE ONLY OPTION I WILL GIVE YOU.
I PROMISE TO KEEP WHAT I'VE LEARNED TO MYSELF FOR NOW.
BUT YOU MUST TRUTHFULLY TELL ME EVERYTHING THERE IS TO KNOW ABOUT SYLTHFARN FROM NOW ON.
OF COURSE, YOUR MAJESTY.

UM...
YOUR NAME WAS MEL?
PLEASE DO CONTINUE TO COME BY MY ROOM TO HAVE TEA WITH ME.
I WOULD LIKE TO GET TO KNOW YOU BETTER.

GO GET SOME REST.
...I'M SO SORR
...
YUE...
...
しゅん

YOU'RE NOT GOING TO MAKE MEL QUIT, ARE YOU?

WHY EVER WOULD I DO THAT?
SHUT

YOU THINK US...
...SO CRUEL?

DRIP

SYLTH...

"SERA-PHIA..."

Waaaaaahh!

Waaaah!

Episode.26
100% PURE CEYLON
ROYAL
ASSAM
TEA

THANKS AGAIN FOR SHARING YOUR ADVICE.
YOU'RE WELCOME!

I COULDN'T TALK ABOUT IT TO JUST ANYONE.
YOU REALLY SAVED THE DAY.
REALLY? THAT'S GREAT.

OKAY.
SEE YOU TOMORROW.
YES, TOMORROW.

STRANGE! I'VE NEVER BEEN ASKED FOR ADVICE BEFORE.
WAS I AT ALL HELPFUL TO LIA?
SIGH
I CAN ONLY HOPE SO!

I'M SURE YOU WERE
SHE THANKED YOU, DIDN'T SHE?

THAT'S TRUE ENOUGH.

YOUR TEA IS SIMPLY THE BEST! ♡
EHEH!

DOESN'T IT SMELL MAR-VELOUS?
MY FRIEND BLENDS THESE ESPECIALLY FOR ME.

DOES HE SELL TEA FOR A LIVING?
I mean, your friend?

NO, NO.
He's a priest.
くす.

WE'VE BEEN BEST FRIENDS SINCE WE MET AT SEMINARY.
HE'S THE ONLY PERSON I BECAME CLOSE TO THERE.
か
ちゃ.

...
......?

I COME FROM A POOR FAMILY. I WAS THE ONLY STUDENT THERE ON A SCHOLARSHIP.

MOST OF THE STUDENTS WERE ARISTOCRATS AND COULDN'T BE TROUBLED TO GIVE ME THE TIME OF DAY. I WAS RESENTED.

AND YET EVEN IN SUCH AN ENVIRONMENT...

...AND DESPITE HIS BEING FROM A VERY, VERY WEALTHY FAMILY...

...HE QUICKLY BECAME MY FRIEND. HE'S A MOST UNUSUAL PERSON.

GLENN! YOU HAVE A VISITOR! ★
ELLO! ELLO! ELLO!
Huh?
Oh.
I TRUST YOU ALL ARE IN EXCELLENT SPIRITS!

I AM A PRIEST FROM THE MESETA CHURCH IN THE EASTERN REGION OF VIEGALD.
ALLOW ME TO INTRODUCE MYSELF. MY NAME IS FRANCIS ZAVIST!
TODAY, I HAVE COME TO SEE...
...Glenn!
Click
WIND
WIND
WIND
WIND
WIND
WHEW!
AND I AM HERE TODAY TO SEE MY ONE AND ONLY FRIEND, GLENN!
Ha ha ha!
IS IT REALLY NECESSARY FOR HIM TO HAVE HIS OWN THEME SONG?
Especially if it has to be operated by hand!

Hee hee.
YOU HAVEN'T CHANGED A BIT!
FRANCIS, IT IS FANTASTIC TO SEE YOU!
He still uses his music box.
OH! GLENN!
Oh!
IT'S BEEN SUCH A LONG TIME!

MUNCH
IT'S SUCH A BEAUTIFU DAY!
むぐ むぐ
EVEN MY HUMBLE BREAD TASTES GOOD!
WHAT'S THIS?
HUH?
ガ
ガッ
YOU'RE NOT EATING IN THE DINING HALL WITH THE OTHERS?
NO.
I CAN'T AFFORD IT.
OH, I SEE!
YOU'RE THE INFAMOUS STUDENT HERE ON SCHOLAR-SHIP!
Mm-hmm.

LOTS OF STUDENTS SAY CRUEL THINGS ABOUT YOU, YOU KNOW.
BUT DON'T WORRY.
EVERYONE IS EQUAL IN THE EYES OF GOD.
WHY...
WHY AREN'T YOU EATING WITH THE OTHERS?
EH?
'CAUSE MY FEAST...
...IS RIGHT HERE!

TEA?
ONE DRINKS TEA IN ORDER TO RELAX.
HOW CAN ONE RELAX ALL COOPED UP IN A STUFFY ROOM?
Care to join me?
I SEE...
EXCELLENT. NOW PAY ATTENTION.
ONE MUST LEARN THE TEA CEREMONY IF ONE HOPES TO GET CLOSER TO GOD.

AND THAT'S HOW WE MET.
WHAT A WONDERFUL FRIEND YOU HAVE.
WHAT?!
Are you serious?
THE GUY'S A NUTCASE!
AHA!
YOU MUST BE THE MASTER WIZARD SYLTHFARN?!
EH?!
WAH!
IT IS A GREAT HONOR ...
... TO ...
... MEET ...
... YOU.
EEP!
BACK OFF!
THE MASTER WIZARD IS MORE IMPORTANT THAN YOU'LL EVER BE.
That was close!
YOU CAN'T JUST UP AND HUG HIM, YOU KNOW.
OH!

PLEASE FORGIVE ME.
FRANCIS. I WAS JUST TALKING ABOUT YOU.
ABOUT YOUR TEA.
SPEAKING OF WHICH ...
WOULD YOU LIKE TO TRY ...
...MY LATEST BLEND?
GLADLY!
Sure!
Weirdo.
Pfft! Pfft! Pfft! Pfft!
GLENN.
STRANGE PEOPLE SURE DO SEEM TO LIKE YOU.
Take Sylth.
You have a point.

?!!
I FOR-
GOT--
Ah.
CLICK
POP
......
POP
GLENN, I NEVER IMAGINED YOU WOULD EVER HAVE A FRIEND LIKE HIM!
?
?
Bravo!
I AM SO HAPPY FOR YOU!

THIS BLEND IS ...

IT'S BEYOND AMAZ ING!

I'VE NEVER TASTED ANYTHING QUITE LIKE THIS.

WELL, ACTU ALLY, I...

IT'S... NOT BAD.

ズズー

WHY AM I JOIN-ING THEM?

Who is this?!

GYA HA HA HA HA HA HA HA HA!

IT'S GETTING DARK NOW.
I SUPPOSE I'D BEST GET GOING.
WHAT? ALREADY?
MM-HMM.
HUH?
....
DOES HE NOT...?
IF YOU INSIST. BUT BEFORE YOU GO...
...I'D LIKE TO GIVE YOU SOME OF MY OWN BLENDED TEA TO TAKE WITH YOU.

OH
LET ME HELP YOU!
かたん。
THANK YOU, MERLE-AWE.
OF COURSE!
UH...
DO YOU REALLY THINK THAT FRANCIS CAME ALL THIS WAY JUST TO HAVE TEA WITH YOU?
EH?
I JUST FEEL THAT HE MIGHT WANT TO TALK TO YOU ABOUT...
...SOME-THING.
YOU THINK...?
COULD FRANCIS HAVE A PRO-BLEM?!

FRAN-CIS.

EH?

IS...

...SOME-THING TROUB-LING YOU?

カチャ

...I'VE FALLEN IN LOVE WITH A WOMAN.
OF COURSE, I'VE DONE NOTHING TO BE ASHAMED OF.
BUT...
...THE CHURCH IN MESETA QUICKLY THREW ME OUT ON MY HEELS.
AH, NO.
I DIDN'T COME HERE FOR A CONSUL-TATION.
I MERELY WANTED TO SEE YOUR FACE SO MUCH!
YOU KNOW HOW I AM.
I HAVE NO TRUE FRIENDS APART FROM YOU.
Ha ha!
FRANCIS...
...I UNDERSTAND.

WHEN YOU'RE DOWN...

...AND FEELING LONELY...

...SEEING SOMEONE SPECIAL CAN BE...

...THE BEST MEDICINE...

...FOR YOUR HEART.

WHEN-EVER YOU WANT TO COME SEE ME...
...PLEASE DO COME SEE ME. ANYTIME.

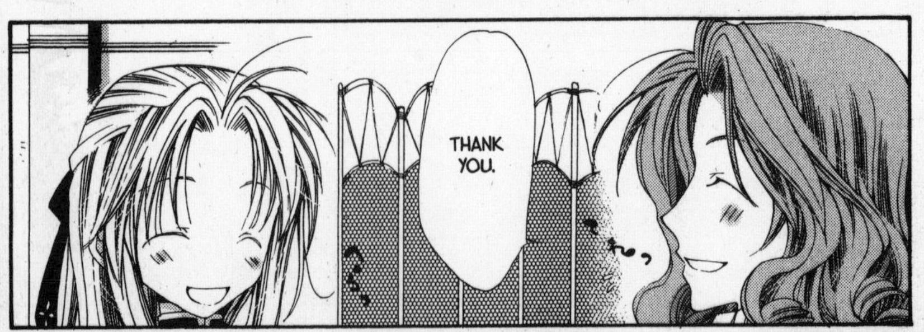

THANK YOU.

THANK YOU VERY MUCH...
... MERLE-AWE.
OH NO!
I JUST THOUGHT ...
...THAT I WANT MY FRIENDS...
...TO BE HAPPY ALL THE TIME!

YES.
I AGREE WITH YOU COMPLETELY.
IF FRANCIS CAN FEEL BETTER BY SIMPLY SEEING MY FACE...
...I MUST GO AND SEE HIM...
...NEXT TIME.
WITH MY NEW TEA.
THAT'S A GREAT IDEA. ♥
WHAT IS THIS STRANGE, UNCOM-FORTABLE AURA?
Is that flowers I see around them?

Episode.27

CINNAMON TASTES LIKE MEDICINE! I HATE IT!

REALLY? BUT APPLE PIE IS NO GOOD WITHOUT IT.

YOU'RE THE ONLY PERSON IN THE WORLD WHO'D EVER EAT A CINNAMON STICK!

IT'S PRETTY GOOD.

Do you want a bite?

This cookie tastes revolting!

....

HEY.
BAD WEATHER GETTING YOU DOWN?

ARE WE...
...CRUEL PEOPLE?
Why ask me that?
WHAT?!

OH. HE'S THINKING ABOUT WHAT THE PRINCESS SAID?
How odd to see him care.
WAS IT A MISTAKE TO HAVE SOMEONE IMPERSONATE SYLTHFARN?

WHY?
IT SHOULD BE A GOOD OMEN THAT WE WERE BLESSED WITH MERLEAWE AND ABLE TO DO IT AT ALL.
SYLTH-FARN...
...MAY NEVER RETURN.

......

SYLTHFARN IS A VERY SMART MAN AND I KNOW NOT WHAT HE INTENDS TO DO.

BUT HE MUST HAVE HAD VERY SERIOUS REASONS TO LEAVE WITHOUT SAYING ANYTHING OF HIS PLANS.

MAYBE WE SHOULD HAVE SEARCHED FOR THE NEXT MASTER WIZARD...

...INSTEAD OF MERELY FINDING AN IMPER-SONATOR.

PERHAPS YOU CAN BE THE NEXT ONE.
I MEAN, AT LEAST FOR NOW...
I'M NOT AS CONFI-DENT AS YOU BELIEVE ME TO BE.
IT'S SYLTH WHO IS TRULY STRONG.

ALL I CAN DO NOW IS TO PREPARE FOR WHAT I EXPECT WILL HAPPEN.

YOU THINK TOO MUCH.

HMM...

SO THIS IS THE MAGICAL KINGDOM OF VIEGALD?

HUH?
NOT TOO SHABBY.
Let's see... ♡
ブ
DID SOME CHILDREN DO THAT TO YOU?
WHAT A CRUEL THING TO DO.

ぐしゃ

TWIST!

♪

SOMEONE'S HERE TO DELIVER SOMETHING HE CLAIMS TO HAVE GOTTEN FROM SYLTHFARN?!
HE'S A WIZARD FROM THE VILATA KINGDOM IN THE SOUTH.
WHO IS THIS GUY? DID HE REALLY SEE SYLTHFARN?
I WILL VERIFY THAT FROM HIM RIGHT NOW.
ALL OF YOU REMAIN IN THE NEXT ROOM, ALL RIGHT?
SYLTH-FARN ...

PLEASE ENTER JUST AS I TOLD YOU, UNDERSTAND?

Y-

YES.

I WONDER WHAT THIS MAN WILL BE LIKE...

FORGIVE ME FOR MAKING YOU WAIT SO LONG.

MY NAME IS YUE ALISTELAFORD AND I AM THE UNDERSECRETARY OF MAGIC.

OH! HOW DO YOU DO!

MY NAM IS ARD AURIS. I'M A WIZARD FROM VILATA.
SO VERY KIND OF YOU TO JOURNEY ALL THIS WAY. SHALL WE BEGIN?
YOU WANT TO SEE WHAT HE GAVE ME, DON'T YOU?
HERE IT IS.
A CLOAK?
WHY?
I HAVE NO IDEA.
I WAS ONLY INSTRUCTED TO BRING IT HERE.
THIS...

THIS DOESN'T BELONG TO SYLTHFARN.
THIS IS DEFINITELY SYLTHFARN'S CLOAK!!
WHAT DO OU MEAN?
CLICK
IT IS IMPOSSIBLE FOR YOU TO HAVE MET THE MASTER WIZARD...
...AS HE HASN'T JOURNEYED FROM THE CASTLE. SEE, HE HAS NEVER LEFT.
YES, I AM VERY MUCH AFRAID THAT YOU MUST HAVE MERELY MET A STRANGER WHO CLAIMED TO BE THE MASTER WIZARD.
FOR THIS IS MASTER WIZARD SYLTHFARN.
I SEE.
A RE-MARKABLE RESEM-BLANCE.
AND YET...

...HE IS QUITE DIFFERENT FROM THE PERSON I MET.
I WILL LEAVE THE CLOAK WITH YOU.
I MUST BE ON MY WAY.

BUT, IN TERMS OF MAGIC...
...YOU ARE NOTHING LIKE HIM.
!!

...

SLAM
THAT MAN!!
Tch.
EVERY-THING GO ALL RIGHT ...
...I HOPE?
ひょい
PLEASE GO AND WAIT FOR ME IN OUR MEETING ROOM.
EH?
WHAT'S THE MATTER WITH YUE?
NO CLUE.
GOOD JOB... MERLEAWE?

DID HE REALIZE THAT I'M NOT THE MASTER WIZARD?!

OH!
I FORGOT SOMETHING!
SWISH
HEY!
YOU CAN'T JUST WALK AROUND WITHOUT--

HEY!!
WHAT'S GOING ON?!
UGH...

WHAT HAP-PENED TO YOU ?!
WHERE DID HE GO?!
!
WHO GOES THERE?!
HELLO, BLEARY-EYED KING!
HOW DID YOU GET IN?!

I SUGGEST YOU COOPER-ATE WITH MY PLAN. ♡
AT ANY RATE, YOU'D BEST JUST LISTEN TO WHAT I HAVE TO SAY.
WHAT?!
?!
MY BODY DOUBLE?!
WHO ARE YOU?!
HE KILLED A HAHZE SO VERY EASILY?!
HUH?
SOME-ONE'S COMING WHO WANTS TO SPOIL MY FUN.

ザァ…

I KNEW YOU'D COME.
YOU SAID...
...YOU WERE THE UNDER-SECRETARY OF MAGIC?
THAT MEANS THAT YOU ARE NOW THE BEST WIZARD...
...THIS COUNTRY HAS TO OFFER, RIGHT?
WHAT ARE YOU IMPLYING?

...!
THE MASTER WIZARD...
Hee hee.
INDEED, I WAS QUITE SURPRISED TO FIND SYLTHFARN HERE SINCE I KNEW VERY WELL THAT HE SIMPLY SHOULDN'T BE.
BUT...
...EVEN SO, THERE HE WAS...
YOU'RE BEYOND RUDE TO SUBSTI-TUTE HIM...
...WITH SUCH A RANK AMA-TEUR.
I KNOW...
...YOU'RE NOTHING SPECIAL, EITHER.

IT WOULD BE SO EASY FOR ME...
...TO TAKE OVER THIS COUNTRY WHERE SYLTHFARN DOESN'T EXIST.
VOOOM

!!
Heh.
IT'S NO USE.
THAT CHARM!!

UGH!!

ズ!!
CLUNK
ISN'T IT REMARKABLE HOW ONE WIZARD CAN TAKE OVER AN ENTIRE MAGICAL KINGDOM...
...ALL BY HIMSELF?

Episode.28

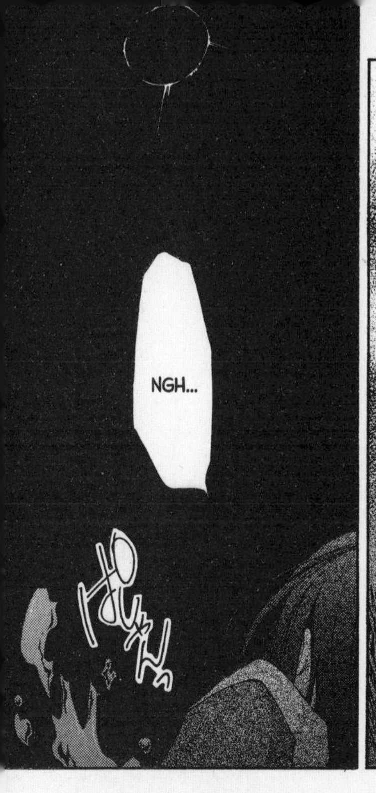
NGH...
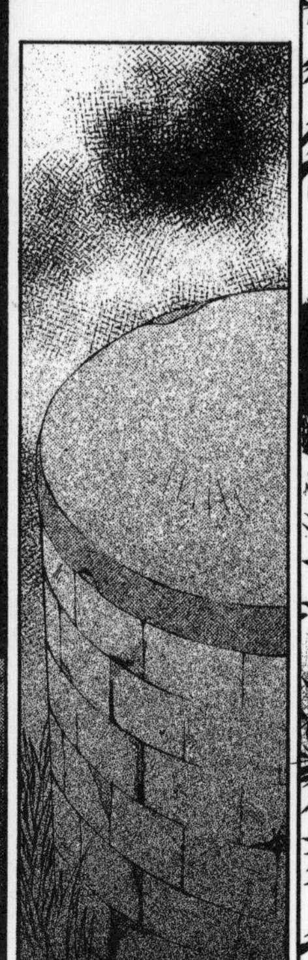

I'M DOWN PRETTY DEEP...

I CAN'T USE MY MAGIC. HE MUST HAVE PLACED A BARRIER AROUND THE WELL.

TMP

Sigh

WHAT AM I GOING TO DO?

Tch!

HELLO!
SYLTH!
YOU'RE LATE!
PLEASE FORGIVE ME!
AH!
LEANNA!
I'LL TAKE CARE OF EVERYTHING BY MYSELF TODAY.
EH?
PLEASE GO AND RELAX IN THE OTHER ROOM.

WHA?
NO, PRINCESS!
ぱたん。
No! I can't allow you to do that yet!
You cannot be alone with him just yet!
IT IS FAR TOO SOON FOR THE TWO OF YOU--
WH-WHAT'S GOING ON? I THOUGHT IT WAS JUST AN AFTERNOON TEA PARTY.
CLK
I WONDER IF IT WAS ALL RIGHT TO LEAVE POOR LEANNA LIKE THAT.
MEL, I WOULD LIKE TO ASK YOU ABOUT SOME-THING.
PLEASE BE HONEST WITH ME. DO YOU KNOW THAT MY GRAND-FATHER ...
Y-YES!
...ALSO HAS SOMEONE TO SERVE AS HIS DECOY?

THE KING?
A DECOY?
EH?
I'M SORRY, BUT I DON'T KNOW. I'VE NEVER HEARD OF SUCH A THING, THOUGH ...
WHY DO YOU ASK?
MY GRAND-FATHER IS ACTING STRANGELY.
HE JUST TOLD ME THAT HE'S BREAKING OFF MY ENGAGE-MENT TO SYLTH-FARN.
BREAKING OFF YOUR ENGAGE-MENT?!
WHAT'S GOING ON, GRAND-FATHER?!

IS IT TRUE THAT YOU WISH TO BREAK OFF MY ENGAGEMENT...
...TO SYLTH-FARN?!
MY DECISION IS MADE.
EXPLAIN TO ME WHY!
PLEASE!!
SLAP
EEK!
EH?!

SILENCE! GO TO YOUR ROOM IMMEDIATELY...
GRAND-FATHER?!
...SERA-PHIA!
HE'S NEVER HIT ME BEFORE LIKE THAT. NEVER!
AND HIS FACE WAS...

I'VE NEVER SEEN SUCH A SCARY SIDE OF MY GRANDFATHER BEFORE.
HE MUST BE VERY SERIOUS ABOUT THIS.
WHAT AM I TO DO?
HE'S USUALLY SO GENTLE.
COULD THAT KIND KING TRULY DO SUCH A HORRIBLE THING TO HER?!
THERE MUST BE SOME KIND OF EXPLANATION.
THERE'S NO WAY THAT HE WOULD BEHAVE THAT WAY WITHOUT GOOD REASON.
I...
I HOPE SO...
OH, I SEE...

wheeze
wheeze
THANK YOU, KING.
I UNDERSTAND EVERYTHING ABOUT YOUR COUNTRY NOW.
BY THE WAY, EVEN I COULD FEEL WHAT AN AMAZING MAN SYLTHFARN WAS TO EVERYONE.
I'M GLAD THAT I DEFEATED YUE FIRST.
Heh.
I HATE THAT KIND OF PERSON.
NOTHING COULD BE MORE OBNOXIOUS.

NOW...
...WHAT SHALL I DESTROY NEXT?

HUH?

JUST THE TWO OF YOU HERE?
Hello!

VAITH'S SO BORING.
PLEASE DON'T FIGHT.
HOW ELSE SHOULD WE ENTERTAIN YOU, THEN?

JUST NOW, I SAW A WHOLE SLEW OF PEOPLE FROM THE MAGICAL DEPARTMENT LOOKING FOR YUE UPSTAIRS.
HAVE YOU SEEN HIM TODAY?

NO.
DID YOU?
NO, I SURE HAVEN'T.
THAT'S STRANGE.
HAS HE GOT A WOMAN?
EH?

A WOMAN?!
DEAR YUE! PLEASE STAY WITH ME A LITTLE LONGER!
BUT I HAVE A VERY IM-PORTANT JOB.
YOU'RE RIGHT. I CAN'T BE SELFISH!
BUT I LOVE YOU SO!
SOB

I'M OFF TO WORK NOW.

YOU'RE DISGUST-ING.
......
Get me away from here.

CAPTAIN VAITH!!
HM?
HEY!
WHAT'S GOING ON?
You...
YOU MUST COME WITH ME AT ONCE!
THE TRUTH IS...
WH...?!
WHAT DID YOU SAY?!

HEY!!

WHAT THE HELL ...
...ARE YOU GUYS DOING ?!
AND YOU!
WHY HAS NOBODY STOPPED THEM?!
Tch!
Man...
Those Fools!
OH MY GOD !!

!
ARE YOU ALL RIGHT?!
UNH...
THIS ISN'T GOOD. THAT CUT IS AWFULLY DEEP.
SEND FOR A DOCTOR!

PLEASE EXPLAIN TO ME HOW THIS HAPPENED.
THEY TOLD ME...
...THAT YOU ORDERED THEM TO KILL ONE ANOTHER.
WHAT ?!
CHIEF, WHAT ARE YOU TALKING ABOUT?!
....
WHY WOULD I GIVE SUCH AN ORDER TO MY MEN?!
FURTHER-MORE...

...I WASN'T EVEN THERE! I WAS BROUGHT TO THE SCENE BY A SOLDIER!

AND YET ALL OF YOUR MEN...

...HAVE TESTIFIED THAT IT WAS YOUR ORDER!

WHA--

WHAT THE HELL?!

DO YOU REMEMBER WHAT YOU SAID TO ME?!

CERTAINLY, SIR.

WE SIMPLY FOLLOWED THE ORDERS OF YOU, OUR LEADER.

......

VAITH!

I'LL HAVE TO TAKE YOU INTO CUSTODY.

COOL YOUR HEAD ON THE COLD DUNGEON FLOOR.

ばっ

G---

GUYS!

VAITH! VAITH!!

HE'S IN JAIL!
HIS OWN MEN!
Uh...
Uh...
Uh...
HE HURT THEM! THE ORDER!

MEL! CALM DOWN!
You're not making sense.
Y--
Yes.
ぽ

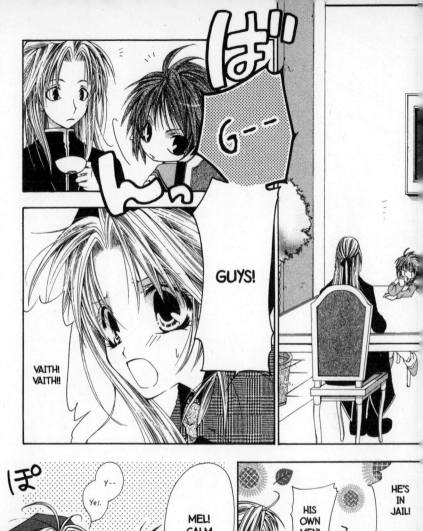

I WAS JUST NOW TOLD THAT...
...VAITH HAS BEEN TAKEN INTO CUSTODY BY THE CHIEF OF THE BLACK KNIGHTS! HE'S LOCKED AWAY INSIDE A BASEMENT PRISON CELL...
...B-BECAUSE HE ORDERED HIS MEN TO KILL EACH OTHER!
......

DON'T YOU THINK YOU GUYS WENT A BIT TOO FAR?
HURTING ONE OF OUR OWN MEN JUST SO YOU COULD SEND ME TO JAIL?

VAITH ORDERED HIS MEN TO KILL EACH OTHER?
THAT'S IMPOS-SIBLE.
WHO IS...
...MANIP-ULATING MY MEN?
I DON'T UNDER-STAND.
WHY ARE THESE TERRIBLE THINGS HAPPENING?

HAVE YOU HEARD?
.....
THEY SAY HE WAS PERFORMING BIZARRE RITUALS WITH THE CHILDREN!
IT'S SO SCARY...
OH YES.
EVERYONE'S HEARD ABOUT THAT WARPED PRIEST.
ISN'T IT DISGUST-ING?!
APPEARANCES CAN BE DECEIVING.
INDEED.

Episode.29

...!

WHAT?

WHO POSTED THIS OUT THERE?!
I DON'T KNOW!

PEOPLE ARE IGNORANT TO JUDGE A PERSON BY WHAT THEY READ ON A STUPID PIECE OF PAPER LIKE THIS.
No good!
A...
ANY-WAYS!

WE MUST GO...

...TALK TO GLENN!

I'M AFRAID UNTIL THE MATTER IS RESOLVED, WE CAN'T ALLOW HIM TO SEE ANYONE.
PLEASE!
I ONLY NEED A LITTLE TIME WITH HIM!
PLEASE!
HM...
WELL, OKAY...
I WILL ALLOW YOU TO SPEAK WITH HIM, BUT ONLY THROUGH THE DOOR.
OVER THERE. GO STAND BY IT.

THANK YOU SO MUCH!
Thanks.
KNOCK
GLENN?
KNOCK KNOCK
Glenn?

MER-LEAWE...
...YOU SHOULDN'T HAVE COME HERE.
YOU LOOK TOO MUCH LIKE SYLTHFARN!

IF THEY REALIZE YOU'RE NOT IN THE CASTLE...

BUT!

FRANCIS IS INVESTI-GATING THE SOURCE OF THIS VICIOUS RUMOR.

BUT...

...I FEAR THIS IS MORE THAN JUST MERE SLANDER.
I HAVEN'T SEEN YUE FOR SEVERAL DAYS NOW.
VAITH WAS PUT INTO JAIL.
SOME-THING SINISTER IS AT WORK HERE.

WHAT'S GOING ON?!
FERN?
WHAT THE HELL IS HAP-PENING RIGHT NOW?!
I DON'T UNDER-STAND! PLEASE MAKE ME UNDER-STAND!

I'M SORRY.
BUT I DON'T UNDERSTAND WHAT'S GOING ON, EITHER.
YOU KNOW, I CAN'T UNDER STAND...
...WHAT THE REST OF YOU THINK'S SO GREAT ABOUT LOVE.

I SIMPLY DON'T UNDERSTAND ANYTHING ABOUT...
...LOVING OR BEING LOVED.
...

Ardi, I like you.

...

EVEN AS A CHILD, I UNDERSTOOD NOTHING OF A GIRL'S CHILDISH AFFECTIONS.

AND SO I HIT HER VERY HARD IN THE FACE.

SHE STARTED CRYING WITH A SAD, TWISTED EXPRESSION.

I FOUND IT FUNNY!
I LAUGHED SO HARD.

YOUR SON'S MAGICAL POWERS ARE NOT NORMAL.

THEY HAVE BANKRUPT-ED HIS EMOTIONS.

YOU SHOULD SEND HIM TO A PROPER FACILITY TO TEACH HIM A SENSE OF ETHICS.

ALTHOUGH THERE WAS NOTHING WRONG WITH ME, ADULTS ALWAYS SAID BAD THINGS ABOUT ME.
AND SO I LEFT HOME.

IT WAS NOT DIFFICULT FOR ME TO SURVIVE.
MY POWER HELPS ME A LOT.
BUT THEN, ONE DAY...
BOY...

INDEED, YOU DO HAVE A VERY DIFFERENT DESTINY THAN MOST.
YOU HAVE SUCH STRONG POWER.
AND YET, BAD THINGS WILL HAPPEN TO YOU IN TIME.
I WAS SO MAD AT HER, I KILLED HER RIGHT THEN AND THERE.
IT WAS THE FIRST TIME I EVER KILLED A PERSON.
BUT I DIDN'T FEEL ANYTHING.

I MET SYLTHFARN ABOUT FOUR MONTHS AGO.

SINCE IT WAS THE VERY FIRST TIME I'D EVER ENCOUNTERED ANYBODY WITH A SIMILAR LEVEL OF POWER TO MINE...

...I REMEMBER HIM RATHER WELL.

I LEARNED THAT HE W FROM TH MAGICAL KINGDOM VIEGALD.

I THOUGHT, HOPED, THAT THERE WOULD BE LOTS OF PEOPLE LIKE ME ...

...IN THE KINGDOM.

THAT'S WHY I DECIDED TO COME HERE.

I...
...DON'T UNDER-STAND ANYTHING ANYMORE.
....
HOW COULD SYLTH NOT BE HERE AT SUCH A CRUCIAL TIME?
THE MASTER WIZARD?

WHAT WOULD HE DO IN THIS SITUA-TION?
HMM, FIRST, I THINK HE WOULD TRACK DOWN YUE!
Find Out!!
AND HE'D SOMEHOW PERSUADE THAT STUBBORN CHIEF TO RELEASE VAITH.
Talking.
blah blah

HE'D ALSO FIND OUT WHY THE KING WAS ACTING SO STRANGE AND EVERYTHING!
ONE WORD FROM HIM AND PEOPLE WOULD DISMISS THAT RIDICULOUS RUMOR ABOUT GLENN, TOO.
Command.

MEAN-WHILE, I AM USELESS.

AHHH!!

THIS IS IMPOS-SIBLE!
I SIMPLY CAN'T TAKE CARE OF THINGS IN THE SAME EXACT WAY THAT THE MASTER WIZARD WOULD!
HEREFORE, MUST DO WHAT I CAN DO!
?!
WHAT ARE YOU TALKING ABOUT, MEL?
WHA?!
YOU? WHAT CAN YOU DO?!

LET'S...
ぎゅっ
...THINK TOGETHER!
IT'LL BE ALL RIGHT.
SURELY, THERE MUST BE SOME THING...
...WE CAN DO!

カタ
カタ
カタ

ALL RIGHT...
GUESS IT'S MORE PRODUCTIVE THAN COMPLAINING.
ぱっ

SO FIRST, ALL OUR ADULTS ARE USELESS.
I know. Forgive me.

AND I FEAR YOU CAN'T DO ANYTHING BY YOURSELF.

THAT'S RIGHT!
Come! Let's do this together!

NOT TO POSE AS THE MASTER WIZARD...

...BUT INSTEAD, TO SERVE AS MYSELF...

...BY DOING WHATEVER I CAN DO.

ふわっ
OH, SWELL.
YOU GUYS ARE GIVING UP THE FIGHT ALREADY?

MM-HMM.
I SEE I SHOULD HAVE GONE FAR EASIER ON YOU.
NOW I'LL NEVER GET TO HEAR...
...WHAT YOU THOUGHT OF MY MARVEL-OUS SKILLS.
ho
AND THEY THOUGHT I WASN'T PAYING ATTENTION IN SCHOOL!

NOW, TELL ME!
Ugh ...
WHO PUT YOU UP TO POSTING THESE PAPERS?
Glenn is my best friend!

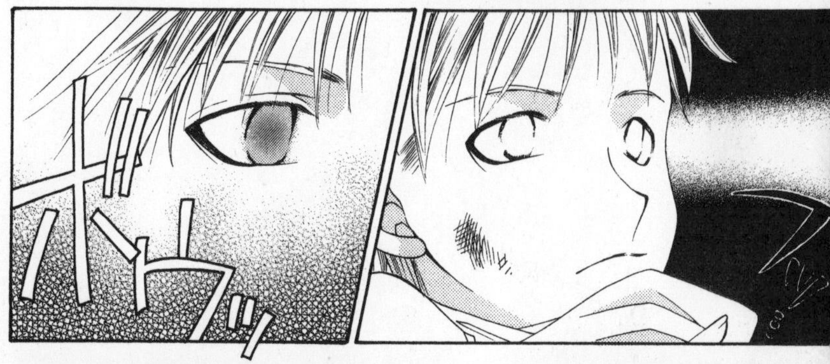

HUH?
WHAT?

WHAT'S WRONG WITH YOU?!
SLAP SLAP SLAP SLAP SLAP
HEY!

WHAT IN THE WORLD IS GOING ON? WHAT IS THIS?
THEY'RE BEHAVING LIKE DOLLS.
......

WHAT IN THE WORLD IS GOING ON? WHAT IS THIS?

THEY'RE BEHAVING LIKE DOLLS.

OH!
I'M RUNNING OUT OF TIME!

VAITH WAS THROWN IN JAIL.
GLENN WAS PLACED UNDER HOUSE ARREST FOR SOMETHING HE DIDN'T DO.
AND WHERE IS YUE IN THIS CRAZI-NESS?
WHAT'S REALLY GOING ON?!

CAUTION
Episode.30

HELLO?
ARE YOU FRIENDS OF GLENN?
OH!
TWIST TWIST
HI! YOU'RE THAT HAHZE BOY!
WHO IS SHE?
N...
Nice to meet you!
FRANCIS.
DID YOU FIND OUT ANYTHING?
MM-HMM.

I CONFRONTED THE YOUNG MEN WHO POSTED THOSE NASTY PAPERS ALL OVER TOWN.
BUT THEY WERE... UNABLE TO ANSWER MY QUESTIONS.

THEY DIDN'T SEEM NORMAL.
IN FACT, I DON'T THINK THEY WERE ALL THERE!
IT SEEMED THEY WERE UNDER SOME KIND OF HYPNOSIS.

WHAT KIND OF NONSENSE IS THIS? WHERE IS YOUR PROOF?
ADMIT-TEDLY, IT WAS ONLY A HUNCH.
HUH?
ONLY A HUNCH?
FOOL! THEN WHY'D YOU EVEN BRING IT UP?!
......
DON'T UNDER-ESTIMATE THE POWER OF A HUNCH.

ANYWAYS, DO YOU HAVE SOME-THING BETTER?
ACTUAL-LY, I HEARD ...
...EVERY BLACK KNIGHT BELIEVES THEY GOT THEIR ORDERS FROM VAITH.
REAL-LY?
EH?!
VAITH IS SO HIGHLY RESPECTED BY HIS MEN!
Besides, Vaith would never order such a thing!
THAT'S UNEXPLAIN-ABLE!
I'M LOCKING UP NOW, SO YOU ALL WILL HAVE TO LEAVE.
IF WE MUST.
GLENN, I'LL SEE YOU TOMOR-ROW.
CLICK

EVERY-ONE...
...PLEASE BE CAREFUL OUT THERE.
LET'S GO!
MEL!
O...
OKAY!
HEY, FERN.
WHAT?

HYPNOTISM MEANS CONTROLLING PEOPLE, RIGHT?

YEAH.

BUT WOULDN'T IT BE HARD TO CONTROL SO MANY PEOPLE AT THE SAME TIME?

OF COURSE.

THOUGH BOTH YUE AND SYLTHFARN COULD DO IT.

TOO BAD YOU CAN'T, MEL.
Thanks for reminding me.
UNFORTU-NATELY, WE CAN'T FIND EITHER ONE OF THEM.
I KNOW.

THEN...
...?
WAH!
WHAT THE?!
YOU CAN PASS THROUGH, BUT I CAN'T?
AH, THERE MUST BE A BARRIER HERE DESIGNED TO PREVENT STRONG MAGICAL POWER FROM PASSING.
SEE! EVEN I'M STRONGER THAN YOU!
MY MAGIC IS BETTER!
I'd better not answer back.
HMM...

WE HAVE TO SPLIT UP.
I'LL LOOK FOR AN ENTRANCE I CAN PASS THROUGH.
MEL, YOU TRY TO NEGOTIATE AND GET VAITH OUT OF PRISON!
OR LOOK FOR YUE.
UM...
OKAY, BUT...
!...
RELAX! IT'S FINE!

MEL!

COME ON, I KNOW YOU CAN DO IT!

...!

WHAT?!

WHERE'S YOUR PROOF?

Proof?

I HAVE A HUNCH.

HEH.

I'LL FIND YOU AS SOON AS I CAN!

ALL RIGHT.

I'LL BE...
...WAITING FOR YOU INSIDE.

きょろ
きょろ
LET'S SEE...
NOW, WHICH WAY TO VAITH'S CELL?
MASTER WIZARD.
ビクッ
WHY...
...ARE YOU HERE?
UH...
WELL...
じりっ
VAITH...

OUR LEADER HAS BEEN...
...SUSPENDED.
R-RE...
REALLY?
?!!
THEN...
I WILL COME BACK AGAIN ANOTHER TIME!
EEK!
WHY...
...ARE YOU RUNNING AWAY FROM ME?
WHY...
...ARE YOU CHASING ME?!

......!

WAH!

I'M SCARED!

WHERE IS THE WAY OUT?!

I MUST RUN FASTER!

THANK GOD!

Sob!

ぱたん
WOW ...
huff
THAT BLACK KNIGHT WAS SURE ACTING STRANGE!
ぽ
ぽ
WHAT AM I GONNA DO?!
I can't get any closer to Vaith.
HMM.
tmp
パラッ
ぱしゃんっ
WHO'S THERE?!
?!

EH?!

DID I JUST HEAR SOMEBODY CALLING OUT FROM THE WELL?!

WAIT, HOLD ON!

ERGH!

It's so heavy!

Y...

YUE?!

HOW EVER DID YOU GET DOWN THERE?!

ARE YOU BY YOURSELF, MERLEAWE?

YES!
VAITH AND GLENN ARE IN TROUBLE.
AND FERN IS--
IT WAS THAT MAN!

"THAT MAN"?

DO YOU REMEMBER THE MAN WHO BROUGHT SYLTHFARN'S CLOAK THE OTHER DAY?

HE'S TRYING TO TAKE OVER OUR COUNTRY!

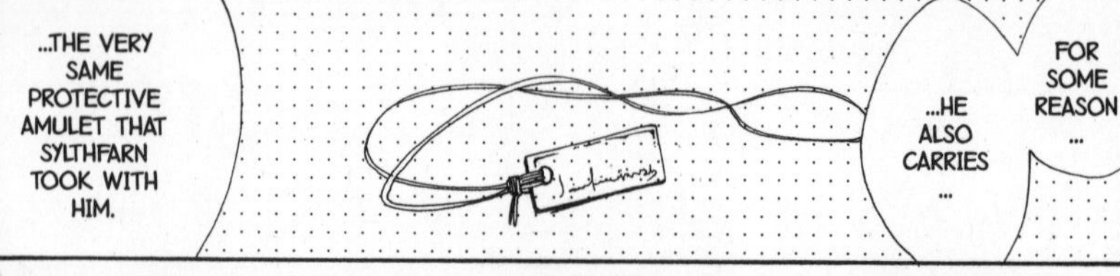

WAIT, MER-LEAWE!
IT IS FAR TOO DANGEROUS FOR YOU TO RETURN TO THE CASTLE BY YOURSELF!
DAMN!
UM...
cough

I SEE RAGS...
...A BROOM...
...HERE'S A BUCKET...
I NEED SOME-THING ELSE!

OH!
THERE IT IS!
HERE WE ARE!

EH?

THAT MONSTER!!
AND PRINCESS SERAPHIA?!
NO WAY!
EEK!
HYagh!!
OW OW OW!!
I...
I MUST GO TO HER RIGHT NOW!

YOU'RE RESPONSIBLE FOR CHANGING MY GRANDFATHER, AREN'T YOU?

WHAT DID YOU DO WITH MY BODY DOUBLE?

!
DON'T COME ANY CLOSER!
I MEAN IT! I'LL JUMP!
IF YOU EVEN TRY AS SO MUCH AS TOUCH ME!!
GO AHEAD! THAT'S AN EXCELLENT IDEA!
I WAS GOING TO KILL YOU ANYWAYS, SO I COULD PIN THE CRIME ON THE MASTER WIZARD.
!
WHAT?
WHAT DID YOU SAY?!

PRINCESS!

I'M ON MY WAY!!

Episode.31

I MUST HURRY! HURRY UP! HURRY!
I MUST GET TO THE PRINCESS AT ONCE!
!!

WHAT FORTUNATE TIMING!

HOW WONDERFUL!

PRINCESS!!

NOW I CAN KILL THE TWO OF YOU TOGETHER.

くす.

WHAT?!

THIS WILL MAKE A GREAT ENDING! THE GRAND FINALE WHERE I STRIKE DOWN THE DERANGED MASTER WIZARD...

...WHO MURDERED POOR PRINCESS SERAPHIA.

How do you like my story so far?

I CAN CREATE WITNESSES AFTER THE FACT!

I'LL HAVE TO TAKE YOU INTO CUSTODY.

COOL YOUR HEAD ON THE COLD DUNGEON FLOOR.

WE SIMPLY FOLLOWED THE ORDERS OF YOU, OUR LEADER.

LEAVE HER ALONE! RIGHT NOW!!
きょと…
Heh.
AH HA HA HA!
SURE, THEY MAY NEED YOU NOW, BUT YOU'LL BE USELESS THE VERY MOMENT THE REAL MASTER WIZARD RETURNS.
WHAT CAN YOU DO? AREN'T YOU A LOWLY OUTSIDER, ANYWAY?
WHY SHOULD OU TRY SO HARD TO PROTECT THESE PEOPLE?

LISTEN...
AGREE TO LEAVE THIS COUNTRY RIGHT NOW AND NEVER RETURN, AND I'LL LET YOU LIVE.
THE FACT IS...
...I DON'T CARE WHO I PIN THIS CRIME ON.
PLEASE RUN AWAY!
MEL!
PLEASE...
THE SUBSTI-TUTE!
THAT IS WHO I AM!

SURE, I MAY BE JUST THE SUBSTI- TUTE...
...AND THEY MAY NOT CARE WHO THAT SUBSTI- TUTE IS.
BUT!
I CARE!
ALL THESE PEOPLE ARE MPORTANT O ME NOW!
AND I WILL HELP THEM!

DO YOU MEAN TO SAY THAT YOU ACTUALLY LIKE THEM?

WHAT CAN YOUR LOVE DO FOR YOU? WILL YOU GET ANY STRONGER?

Stronger than me?

I THINK NOT. YOU'RE A JOKE. AND EVEN IF YOU HAD THE POWER TO MATCH ME...

Heh heh.

...NOTHING WILL WORK AGAINST ME AS LONG AS I HAVE THIS AMULET.

THIS VERY CHARM THAT I SNATCHED AWAY FROM YOUR MASTER WIZARD!

EVEN POOR YUE PROVED POWERLESS AGAINST IT!

cough

AN AMULET?

SYLTH'S AMULET?

HOW AMAZ-ING!

ISN'T IT?

SO THIS TINY ANCIENT TRINKET WILL PROTECT YOU FROM EVERY MAGICAL POWER IN THE WORLD?

WHAT IF SOMEBODY STOLE IT FROM YOU? THAT'D BE BAD!

Ha ha ha

YOU WOULD THINK SO, RIGHT?

BUT THE ANCIENT PEOPLE WERE MOST CLEVER!

THEY PROTECTED THE AMULET WITH A SPELL THAT PREVENTS ANYONE WHO STEALS IT FROM USING IT.

WHAT KIND OF SPELL?

WELL ...

MEL
IT'S A FLOWER!
USE YOUR FLOWER MAGIC!! AGAINST HIM!!
EH?!
WHAT?!
FLOWER?
UM...
ふわっ

WHAT
THIS
CELE-
BRATING
YOUR
DEATH?
Heh
heh.
あーうっ
?!!

WHA?
WHAT'S THIS?!
URK!
Gack!

EEK!!
PRINCESS!

OH...!
NO!
NOOOO!!

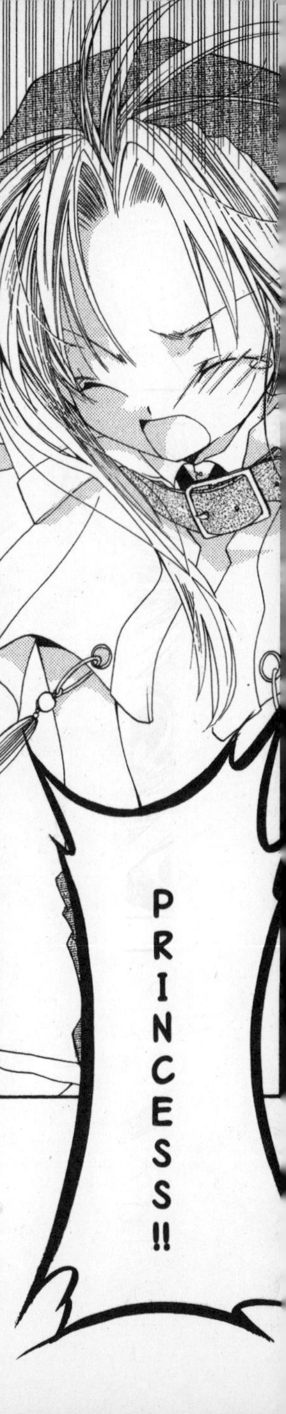
PRINCESS!!

FORGIVE ME FOR CAUSING YOU SUCH TERRIBLE TROUBLE, MEL.
OH...

SYLTH, I'LL NEVER SEE YOU AGAIN...
I MISS YOU.
I WANTED TO SEE YOU AGAIN!

YOU'RE SUCH A TOMBOY!
YOU SHOULDN'T LET YOURSELF FALL FROM SUCH A HIGH PLACE...
...PRINCESS SERAPHIA!

I ASKED YOU TO ALWAYS CALL ME BY MY NAME...
こん
........?!
Huh?

D...
DAMN IT!
ぱたた
THAT DAMN KID!
I'M GOING TO KILL YOU!
HA HA! HA HA HA!

FERN.
YES!
JUST KEEP SUPPORTING MY BODY, OKAY?
WHAT ?!

YOU SWINE!

WHERE DID YOU MEET SYLTH-FARN?!

WHERE IS HE RIGHT NOW?!

AM I TRULY DEFEAT ED...
...BY YOU WORTH-LESS LITTLE PEOPLE?!
......
THIS IS SUCH A BORING ENDING!
HA HA HA...
JUST LIKE HIM...
"HIM"?

WHO IS "HE"?!
WH... WHAT DID YOU SAY?!
?

HEY.

WHAT'D HE SAY, YUE?

...SYLTHFARN
IS DEAD?

Main Character (14 years old)
Merleawe
Silver-white hair
Light blue eyes
She enjoys sweets.
甘党。

MY TIME DOESN'T CORRESPOND WITH THAT OF OTHER PEOPLE.

IT HAS ALWAYS PASSED FASTER THAN THAT OF OTHERS.

I MADE FRIENDS OF MANY AGES...

...TO OBSCURE THE DIFFERENCE.

Episode.32

THIS PERSON ...
...WAS BORN UNDER A VERY INFLUENTIAL STAR.
BUT ITS BRILLIANCE IS ONLY MATCHED BY ITS BREVITY.
MOST LIKELY, THIS PERSON WILL DIE BEFORE HE EVEN BECOMES AN ADULT.
MAY ASK ...
...WHO THIS MAN IS?
I HOPE I CAN TRUST YOU TO KEEP A SECRET.
SADLY, THE STAR I ASKED ABOUT WAS YUE'S.

WHAT ?!
THE UNDER-SECRE-TARY OF THE MAGIC DEPART-MENT?!

DON'T WOR-RY.
I WON'T TELL HIM.
CLATTER

PLUS, HE'S ALREADY ...
...OVER 20 YEARS OLD.
......

SHE'S THE ONLY FORTUNE TELLER IN THE ENTIRE KINGDOM OF VIEGALD THAT THE KING TRUSTS.
OF COURSE, HER BATTING AVERAGE IS WONDERFUL.
I CAN'T TELL HER THAT SHE JUST READ MY FORTUNE.
Especially the ending...

I WONDER...
HOW LONG DO I HAVE TO LIVE?
SYLTH-FARN.
HUH?
I WOULD VERY MUCH LIKE TO DISCUSS WITH YOU THAT TOPIC OF A PERSONAL NATURE THAT WE SPOKE OF EARLIER THIS WEEK...

OH!
I WOULD LIKE YOU TO TAKE CARE OF THE MATTER!
Hey!
LACKEY

AGAIN?

YOU MUST SEVERELY DISLIKE ME TO BURDEN ME WITH YOUR MOST UNPLEAS-ANT TASKS.

Eh heh.

NO, THAT'S NOT WHY I DO IT.

I just don't get it.

INSTEAD, IT MEANS THAT I TRUST YOU...
Hmph!
Hmph!
Hmph!
Hmph!
...YUE.

HEY! SYLTH!
HELLO! VAITH!
IS HE GOOFING OFF AGAIN?!
HOW WAS YOUR PRAC-TICE?
DOESN'T HE KNOW HE'S THE MASTER WIZARD?
DOESN'T HE KNOW HE'S THE CAPTAIN OF THE BLACK KNIGHTS?

LOUSY! I'M TOO STRONG FOR THEM. I DON'T HAVE ANYBODY TO FIGHT AGAINST.

Eh heh heh.

IN FACT, I'M SERIOUSLY CONSIDERING NOT ATTENDING PRACTICE AGAIN UNTIL THEY'RE READY FOR ME.

VAITH IS ALWAYS...

...HIDING BEHIND THE PERSONA OF...

It's boring to have no enemies!

...SMART ALECK OR BAD BOY.

WHAT?
WHAT'S WRONG?
HUH?
EVEN SO, I STILL LIKE HIM.

The difference is 30 cm!
I JUST REALIZED YOU'RE REALLY TALL.

......

PAT
I USED TO...

...BE YOUR HEIGHT WHEN I WAS YOUNGER.
I GOT PICKED ON BECAUSE I WASN'T SKILLED LIKE I AM NOW.
Are you jealous?
I NEVER THOUGHT I'D GET SO TALL.
For some reason, he grates on my nerves.

OH!
SYLTH!!
FERN.
WHAT'S WRONG?
IS HE MAD AT ME?
WHAT NOW?
OH... MAYBE THAT?
COULD HE BE MAD AT ME FOR MIXING GARAM MASALA INTO HIS COCOA?
Get out of my way!
OR MAYBE--
MY...
...COCOA!!

STUPID SYLTH! YOU MADE MY COCOA SPICY!!

He's crying?

BINGO! ☆

OH, MY WORD. I THOUGHT THE COLOR WAS KIND OF STRANGE...

Calm down, Fern.

AH HA HA!

Grr!

WOW!

IF ONLY I COULD HAVE SEEN YOUR FACE WHEN YOU DRANK IT!

Me, too!

IT WAS HILAR-IOUS...

...the way he spat!

HEY!
GLENN! DON'T JUST STAND THERE!
what?
SCOLD SYLTHFARN!

well... but...
......
...
Pfft!
Pfft!
Pfft!
Pfft!
Pfft!

HOW CAN I SCOLD THE MASTER WIZARD?

TRUE, TRUE. HE'S OUR MASTER WIZARD.

THAT'S RIGHT, I'M THE MASTER WIZARD.

ぷ ん

HUH?!
WHAT'S THAT SUP-POSED TO MEAN?!
IT'S NOT FAIR!

Do you really think you can get away with something like that?!
ぷい
I am so sorry!

WE LAUGHED SO HARD TOGETHER.

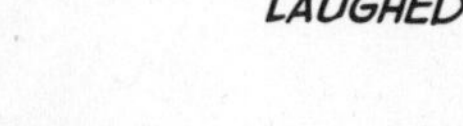

WE LAUGHED...

...UNTIL WE HAD TEARS IN OUR EYES.

What's so funny?

Please, please forgive me, Fern.

Ha ha ha!

HOW MARVELOUS IT WAS...

...TO NAP WITH EVERYONE IN THE SUN.

HOW BLUE THE SKY WAS...

BEING TOGETHER WITH THEM WAS MY GREATEST JOY.
I LOVE YOU ALL!
Continued in Volume 5

Postscript

Hi, this is Mizutani. In volume 4, a villain appeared for the very first time. I sure did enjoy drawing that bad guy a lot! I also got to illustrate a fight scene with Yue! And I got to show Merleawe's serious side. I hope you enjoyed reading this book as much as I liked drawing it!

☆

What is going to happen with Sylthfarn? Yikes, I actually have to think about what will happen to him now. I will do my best to create an interesting story! I'm talking like it's someone else's job.

★

Oh! Thank you for your kind letters and gifts! I'm so very happy to receive them! They are the source of my energy!

★

The fact that you support my work means so very much! I can't thank you enough! And I really do appreciate that you have kept on supporting me. Can't wait to see you in volume 5!

★

2005.01.

Yuzu Mizutani. January 2005

http://mizyuz.cool.ne.jp/
Website: "The Moon Syndrome"

Special thanks to Cherry-chan, Yasuka-chan and Acchi. My friends, my family, my editor and of course everyone in the editorial department!

MAGICAL×MIRACLE
My Timid Story
HI THERE, I AM STILL GROWING OUT MY HAIR AFTER SURVIVING MY DILEMMA.
BOW
HELLO. I'M YUZU MIZUTANI.
Again?
I BOUGHT ...
Hmm, there's a dial switch.
...A CURLING IRON!
I HAVE ALWAYS, ALWAYS WANTED TO HAVE CURLY HAIR!
Okay, I can't do it so well on this side.
GREAT, I'VE FAILED MISERABLY BECAUSE I'M TOO TIMID WHEN I TRY NEW THINGS.
What?
But hello! It's scary to use such a hot iron right by your face! We're talking over 100 degrees Celsius!
Marvelous.
Francis
height → 180cm
hair → Orange Blown
eyes → Violet
blood type → A

YUZU MIZUTANI
My Confession
ALTHOUGH I KNOW THIS IS SUDDEN...
...I WOULD LIKE TO MAKE A CON-FESSION.
scratch scratch scratch scratch scratch scratch scratch scratch scratch
THERE WAS TIME WHEN I WOULD COMPLETELY IGNORE THOSE WHO DARED TRY TO TALK WITH ME.
I RUINED ANY STORY THAT THEY TOLD...
...BY SIMPLY NEVER LISTENING TO THEM.
WHY ARE YOU ALWAYS LIKE THAT?
I'M SORRY NOW.
BRR!
^ ^
Ardi =Auris
height → 170cm
hair → White
eyes → Red
blood type → AB

In the Next Volume of...

Magical × Miracle

Volume 5 Available
July 2007

TOKYOPOP.com

WHERE MANGA LIVES!

JOIN the TOKYOPOP community: www.TOKYOPOP.com

LIVE THE MANGA LIFESTYLE!

CREATE...
UPLOAD...
DOWNLOAD...
BLOG...
CHAT...
VOTE...
LIVE!!!!

WWW.TOKYOPOP.COM HAS:

- Exclusives
- News
- Columns
- Special Features and more...

LEADING THE MANGA REVOLUTION 漫画革命

PSY-COMM © Granger/Henderson/Salvaggio and TOKYOPOP Inc.

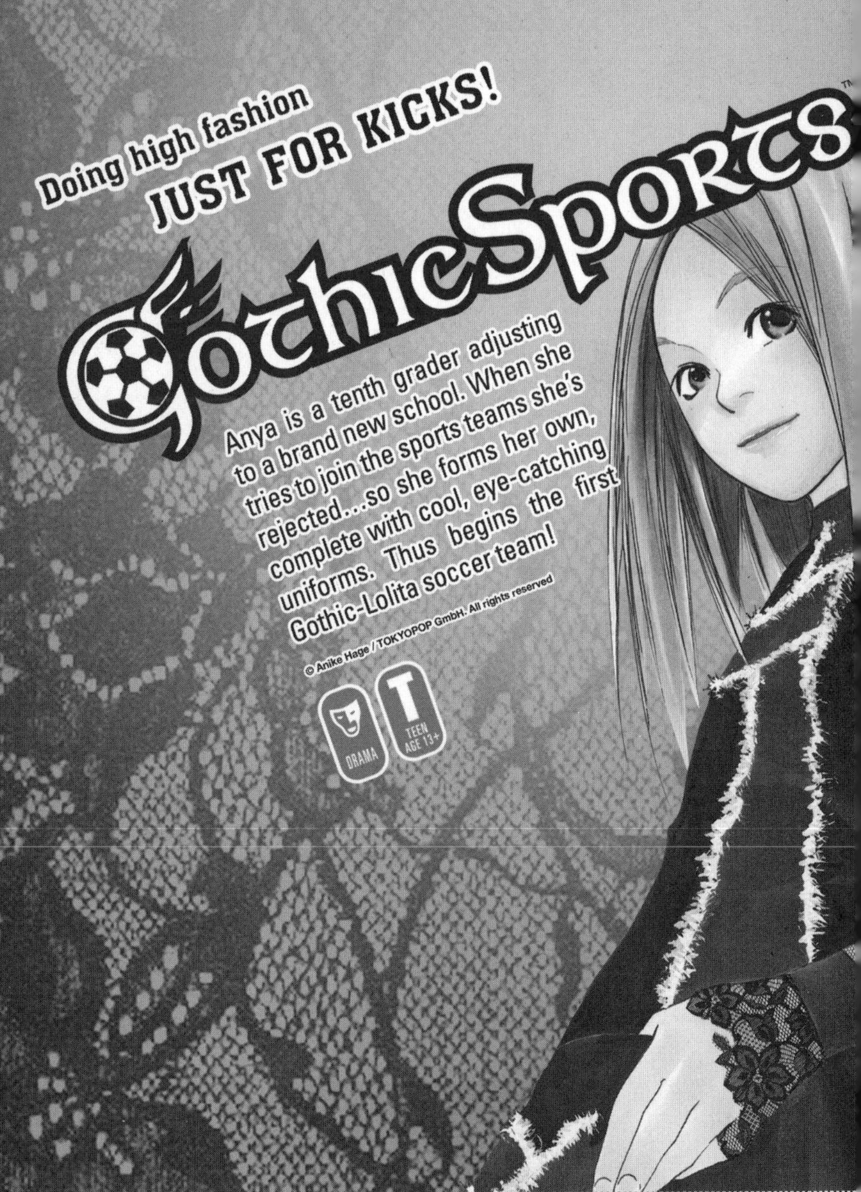

FOR MORE INFORMATION VISIT: WWW.TOKYOPOP.COM

tactics™
Geeky ghost-hunters unite!
Kantarou, a folklore scholar living in the Taisho period, is always broke and always late on his deadlines. But Kantarou moonlights as an exorcist solving the problems of ghosts and demons, all with the help of Haruka, the legendary super-sexy demon-eating tengu!
The manga that influenced the popular anime!
COMEDY
T
TEEN AGE 13+
© SAKURA KINOSHITA and KAZUKO HIGASHIYAMA / MAG Garden.

ERIN HUNTER'S

WARRIORS

THE LOST WARRIOR

What happened to Graystripe?

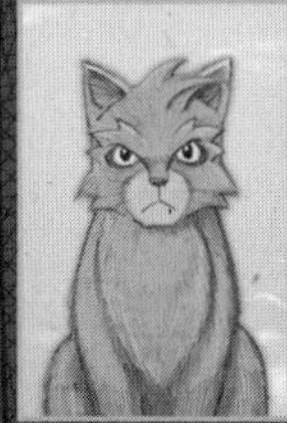

When the Twolegs destroy the warrior clans' forest home, Graystripe—second in command of ThunderClan—is captured while helping his comrades escape! However, he soon discovers that the captive life as a pampered kittypet isn't all that bad. Will Graystripe leave his warrior past behind or answer the call of the wild?

Based on the hit children's series, follow a beloved character's **triumphant return** in manga style!

Available May 2007

HARPER COLLINS & TOKYOPOP

www.WarriorCats.com

Copyright © 2007 by Working Partners Limited. Series created by Working Partners Limited

FOR MORE INFORMATION VISIT: WWW.TOKYOPOP.COM

TOKYOPOP MANGA SUPPLEMENT

Meet Kilala,
an ordinary girl
who loves all the
Disney Princesses!

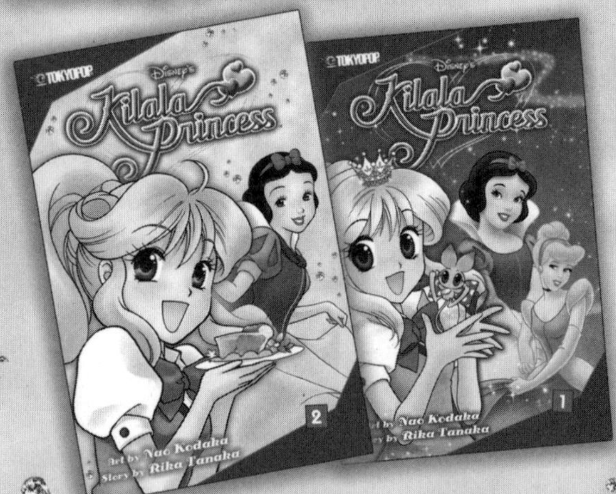

The first manga to capture
the MAGIC of Disney's princesses!

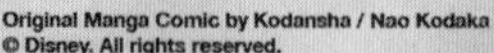
Original Manga Comic by Kodansha / Nao Kodaka
© Disney. All rights reserved.

FOR MORE INFORMATION VISIT: WWW.TOKYOPOP.COM/KILALAPRINCESS

The DARK GOODBYE

A HARDBOILED NOIR SUSPENSE THRILLER GUARANTEED TO LEAVE YOU DEAD!

FROM THE TWISTED MIND OF FRANK MARRAFFINO!
ART BY DREW RAUSCH, CREATOR OF SULLENGREY!

Hired to locate a missing girl, Detective Max "Mutt" Mason discovers deeper malignant forces at work. Femmes fatale soon give way to strange creatures older than humanity, all bent on remaking our world as their own. Mason has questions, but is he ready for the answers?

HORROR

OT
OLDER TEEN AGE 16+

©2007 Frank Marraffino and TOKYOPOP Inc.

FOR MORE INFORMATION VISIT: WWW.TOKYOPOP.COM

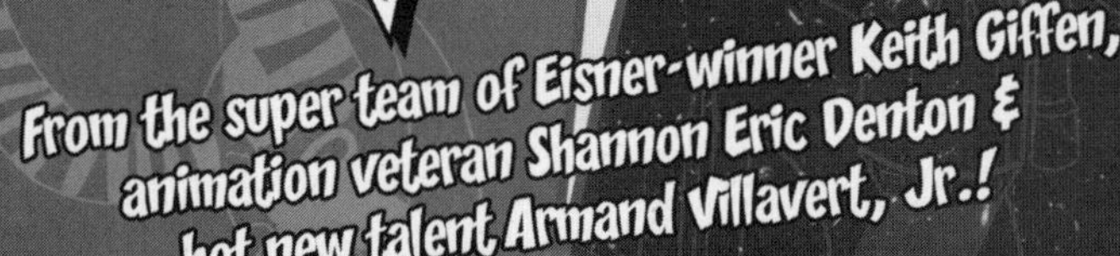

From the super team of Eisner-winner Keith Giffen, animation veteran Shannon Eric Denton & hot new talent Armand Villavert, Jr.!

An exciting heroic manga for 8–12-year-olds!

Twelve-year-old Armand Jones has to police the galaxy and finish his chores all before dinnertime!

Vol. 1 in stores now!
Vol. 2 coming soon!

© Shannon Denton, Keith Giffen and TOKYOPOP Inc.

WWW.TOKYOPOP.COM/MANGAREADERS

SO YOU THINK YOU CAN RHYSMYTH?
RHYSMYTH™
As America's newest and most popular sport, Rhysmyth features one-on-one dance battles atop a hi-tech glass court grid. When the music hits, you and your opponent dance across a digital minefield for the glory of being the fastest, most accurate and stylish Rhysmyther. In steps clumsy high school student Elena looking for a little something extra to beef up her college apps. Now Elena is thrust into the fast-paced world of Rhysmyth, where getting your groove on can lead to rivalry and romance!
DRAMA
T
TEEN AGE 13+
Rhysmyth © Anthony Andora, Lincy Chan and TOKYOPOP Inc

STOP!

This is the back of the book.
You wouldn't want to spoil a great ending!

This book is printed "manga-style," in the authentic Japanese right-to-left format. Since none of the artwork has been flipped or altered, readers get to experience the story just as the creator intended. You've been asking for it, so TOKYOPOP® delivered: authentic, hot-off-the-press, and far more fun!

DIRECTIONS

If this is your first time reading manga-style, here's a quick guide to help you understand how it works.

It's easy... just start in the top right panel and follow the numbers. Have fun, and look for more 100% authentic manga from TOKYOPOP®!